ERIC WHITACRE
COLLECTION

GW00777335

ERIC WHITACRE

Eric Whitacre began singing with his college choir at the age of 18, the experience changing his life forever. He wrote his setting of *Go, Lovely Rose* for that same choir three years later. He gained a Master's degree in Composition at the Juilliard School, where he studied with John Corigliano. Since then, he has received numerous commissioning awards and honours. Performances of his work number in the thousands. A true innovator, he writes music that incorporates contemporary influences and sound vocabulary while demanding the highest standards of precision, intonation, and ensemble. He divides his time between conducting and teaching throughout the world and the ever-increasing demands of his composing. He lives in Los Angeles with his wife, soprano Hila Plitmann, and their son.

LIST OF WORKS

CHESTER MUSIC
part of The Music Sales Group
14/15 Berners Street, London W1T 3LJ, UK.
Telephone: +44 (0)20 7612 7400 Fax: +44 (0)20 7612 7545
Exclusive distributor: **Music Sales Limited**,
Newmarket Road, Bury St Edmunds, Suffolk IP33 3YB, UK.
Telephone: +44 (0)1284 702 600 Fax: +44 (0)1284 702592
web: www.chesternovello.com e-mail: music@musicsales.co.uk

A BOY AND A GIRL

Los novios

Tendidos en la yerba
una muchacha y un muchacho.
Comen naranjas, cambian besos
como las olas cambian sus espumas.

Tendidos en la playa
una muchacha y un muchacho.
Comen limones, cambian besos
como las nubes cambian sus espumas.

Tendidos bajo tierra
una muchacha y un muchacho.
No dicen nada, no se besan,
cambian silencio por silencio.

A Boy and a Girl

Stretched out on the grass
a boy and a girl.
Savouring their oranges, giving their kisses
like waves exchanging foam.

Stretched out on the beach
a boy and a girl.
Savouring their limes, giving their kisses
like clouds exchanging foam.

Stretched out underground
a boy and a girl.
Saying nothing, never kissing,
giving silence for silence.

Octavio Paz
English translation by Muriel Rukeyser

A Boy and a Girl is such a tender, delicate, exquisite poem; I simply tried to quiet myself as much as possible and find the music hidden within the words.

E.W.

GO, LOVELY ROSE

Go, lovely rose,
Tell her that wastes her time and me,
That now she knows,
When I resemble her to thee,
How sweet and fair she seems to be.

Tell her that's young,
And shuns to have her graces spied,
That hadst thou sprung
In deserts where no men abide,
Thou must have uncommended died.

Small is the worth
Of beauty from the light retired;
Bid her come forth,
Suffer herself to be desired,
And not blush so to be admired.

Then die! that she
The common fate of all things rare
May read in thee;
How small a part of time they share,
That are so wondrous sweet and fair!

Edmund Waller (1606-1687)

The piece is structured around the cyclical life of a rose, and is connected througout by the opening 'rose motif', a seed that begins on the tonic and grows in all directions before it blossoms, dies and grows again. Each season is represented: spring begins the piece, summer appears at bar 13, autumn at bar 26, winter at bar 39, with spring returning at bar 49. The form is based on the Fibonacci sequence (the pattern found in plant and animal cells divisions) – its fifty-five bars are a perfect Fibonacci number. The Golden Mean appears at bar 34 as all parts are reunited to complete the flower before its final blossom and inevitable cycle of death and rebirth.

Each performance should be approached with the child-like innocence and naivety that allows us to marvel at the return of the rose each spring. The *szforzandos* throughout must be light and gentle.

E.W.

LUX AURUMQUE

Light and Gold

Light,
warm and heavy as pure gold
and the angels sing softly
to the new-born baby.

Lux Aurumque

Lux,
calida gravisque pura velut aurum
et canunt angeli molliter
modo natum.

Edward Esch
Latin translation by Charles Anthony Silvestri

After deciding upon the poem by Edward Esch (I was immediately struck by its genuine, elegant simplicity), I had it translated into the Latin by the celebrated American poet Charles Anthony Silvestri. A simple approach is essential to the success of the work, and if the tight harmonies are carefully tuned and balanced they will shimmer and glow.

E.W.

NOX AURUMQUE

Night and Gold

Gold,
Tarnished and dark,
Singing of night,
Singing of death,
Singing itself to sleep…

And an angel dreams of dawnings, and of war.
She weeps tears of the golden times,
Tears of the cost of war.

O shield!
O gilded blade!
You are too heavy to carry,
Too heavy for flight.

Gold,
Tarnished and weary,
Awaken!
Melt from weapon into wing!
Let us soar again,
High above this wall;
Angels reborn and rejoicing with wings made
Of dawn,
Of gold,
Of dream.

Gold,
Singing of wings,
Singing of shadows…

Nox Aurumque

Aurum,
Infuscatum et obscurum,
Canens noctis,
Canens mortis,
Acquiescens canendo…

Et angelum somnit aurorarum et bellorum,
Sæculorum aurorum fundit lacrimas,
Lacrimas rerum bellorum.

O arma!
O lamina aurata!
Gestu graves nimium,
Graves nimium volatu.

Aurum,
Infuscatum et torpidum
Suscita!
Dilabere ex armis in alam!
Volemus iterum,
Alte supra murum;
Angeli renascentes et exultantes ad alas
Aurorarum,
Aurorum,
Somnorum.

Aurum,
Canens alarum,
Canens umbrarum.

Charles Anthony Silvestri

Nox Aurumque (Night and Gold) was written as a sort of 'companion piece' to my *Lux Aurumque* (Light and Gold). I used themes (textual and musical) taken from both *Lux Aurumque,* and my work for music theatre, *Paradise Lost: Shadows and Wings.* By my count, this is my seventh collaboration with poet Charles Anthony Silvestri (*Sleep, Leonardo Dreams of His Flying Machine,* etc.) and it was by far our most challenging. Here is a summation of our process together, recounted by the poet himself.

E.W.

The task of the lyricist is to provide for the composer a text which, on the one hand, gives the composer the material he or she needs to complete the piece according to unique specifications, while, on the other hand, standing alone as a poem in its own right. Writing the Latin text for *Nox Aurumque* was a singular challenge.

First, Eric had already composed much of the musical material; several distinct melodic motifs were already formed and essential to the structure of the piece. Any text I composed had to fit within the parameters of that structure. Eric was very specific about the number of syllables in this line, the necessary word-painting in that line, etc.

Second, Eric had strong ideas about the meaning of the text. He communicated impressionistic images of an angel, the emotions of that angel, and other evocative images, darker than usual for him. My text had to speak to those images in a meaningful way, consistent with Eric's intentions for the piece. It has a distinctly different sound than earlier works, and I wanted my text to be darker, and as different.

Third (and most challenging), the text had to flow effectively in Latin. The Latin had to communicate accurately the images Eric wished to evoke about this angel, all within the already-established framework of the piece. Latin affected the English, and English affected the Latin, in a tug-of-war between meaning and grammar. It had to be singable and employ the kind of vowels and consonants Eric likes to set. (We joked that not every word could end in the lovely and mysterious '-um' sound Eric likes so much – Latin grammar just doesn't work that way, although I became intimately familiar with the many uses of the genitive plural!) And the Latin had to be correct – it had to conform to the rules of Latin grammar – to satisfy my need as a scholar. I had to settle at times for some Latin that strayed from what Cicero might have written, but which stayed certainly within the somewhat looser realm of Medieval usage.

From my perspective as a poet, the Latin language is living, vibrant and malleable; I'm certainly not the first poet to take liberties with canonical rules. No doubt there will be quibblers who will question the choices I have made. I humbly ask these critics to consider the *nodus triplex* with which I was presented, and see this poem for what it is – lyrics to a choral work, not a sequel to the *Aeneid.*

Charles Anthony Silvestri

SLEEP

The evening hangs beneath the moon,
A silver thread on darkened dune.
With closing eyes and resting head
I know that sleep is coming soon.

Upon my pillow, safe in bed,
A thousand pictures fill my head,
I cannot sleep, my mind's aflight;
And yet my limbs seem made of lead.

If there are noises in the night,
A frightening shadow, flickering light;
Then I surrender unto sleep,
Where clouds of dream give second sight.

What dreams may come, both dark and deep,
Of flying wings and soaring leap
As I surrender unto sleep,
As I surrender unto sleep.

Charles Anthony Silvestri

In the winter of 1999 Ms Julia Armstrong, a lawyer and professional mezzo-soprano living in Austin, Texas contacted me. She wanted to commission a choral work from me to be premiered by the Austin Pro Chorus (Kinley Lange, conductor), a terrific chorus with whom she regularly performed.

The circumstances around the commission were amazing. She wanted to commission the piece in memory of her parents, who had died within weeks of each other after more than fifty years of marriage; and she wanted me to set her favourite poem, Robert Frost's immortal *Stopping by Woods on a Snowy Evening*. I was deeply moved by her spirit and her request, and agreed to take on the commission.

I took my time with the piece, crafting it note by note until I felt that it was exactly the way I wanted it. The poem is perfect, truly a gem, and my general approach was to try to get out of the way of the words and let them work their magic. We premiered the work in Austin, October 2000, and it was well received. Rene Clausen gave *Stopping by Woods* a glorious performance at the ACDA National Convention in the spring of 2001, and soon after I began receiving hundreds of letters, emails, and phone calls from conductors trying to get a hold of the work.

And here was my tragic mistake: I never secured permission to use the poem. Robert Frost's poetry has been under tight control from his estate since his death, and until a few years ago only Randall Thompson (*Frostiana*) had been given permission to set his poetry. In 1997, out of the blue, the estate released a number of titles, and at least twenty composers set and published *Stopping by Woods* for chorus. When I looked online and saw all of these new and different settings, I naturally (and naively) assumed that it was open to anyone. Little did I know that, just months before, the Robert Frost Estate had taken the decision to deny any use of the poem, ostensibly because of this plethora of new settings.

After a long battle of legalities back and forth, the Estate of Robert Frost and their publisher, Henry Holt Inc., sternly and formally forbade me to use the poem for publication or performance until the poem would become public domain in 2038.

I was crushed. The piece was dead, and would sit under my bed for the next 37 years as a result of rulings by heirs and lawyers. After many discussions with my wife, I decided that I would ask my friend and brilliant poet Charles Anthony Silvestri (*Leonardo Dreams of His Flying Machine, Lux Aurumque*) to set new words to the music I had already written. This was an enormous task, because I was asking him to not only write a poem that had the exact structure of the Frost poem, but that it would even incorporate key words from *Stopping By Woods*, like 'sleep'. Tony wrote an absolutely exquisite poem, finding a completely different (but equally beautiful) message in the music I had already written.

And there it is. My setting of Robert Frost's *Stopping by Woods* no longer exists. I am supremely proud of this new work, and my only regret in all of this was that I was way too innocent in my assumption that lawyers would understand something as simple and delicate as the choral art.

E.W.

THIS MARRIAGE

May these vows and this marriage be blessed.
May it be sweet milk,
like wine and halvah.
May this marriage offer fruit and shade
like the date palm.
May this marriage be full of laughter,
our every day a day in paradise.
May this marriage be a sign of compassion,
a seal of happiness, here and hereafter.
May this marriage have a fair face and a good name,
an omen as welcomes the moon in a clear blue sky.
I am out of words to describe
how spirit mingles in this marriage.

Jalal ad-Din Rumi (1207-73)
English translation by Kabir Helminski

This Marriage is just a small and simple gift to my wife on the occasion of our seventh wedding anniversary.

E.W.

WATER NIGHT

Agua Nocturna

Water Night

La noche de ojos de caballo que
    tiemblan en la noche,
la noche de ojos de agua en el campo dormido,
está en tus ojos de caballo que tiembla,
está en tus ojos de agua secreta.

Ojos de agua de sombra,
ojos de agua de pozo,
ojos de agua de sueño.

El silencio y la soledad,
como dos pequeños animales a quienes guía la luna,
beben en esos ojos,
beben en esas aguas.

Si abres los ojos,
se abre la noche de puertas de musgo,
se abre el reino secreto del agua
que mana del centro de la noche.

Y si los cierras,
un río, una corriente dulce y silenciosa,
te inuda por dentro, te hace oscura:
la noche moja riberas en tu alma.

Night with the eyes of a horse that
    trembles in the night,
night with eyes of water in the field asleep
is in your eyes, a horse that trembles,
is in your eyes of secret water.

Eyes of shadow-water,
eyes of well-water,
eyes of dream-water.

Silence and solitude,
two little animals moon-led,
drink in your eyes,
drink in those waters.

If you open your eyes,
night opens, doors of musk,
the secret kingdom of the water opens
flowing from the centre of night.

And if you close your eyes,
a river, a silent and beautiful current,
fills you from within, flows forward, darkens you
night brings its wetness to beaches in your sou

Octavio Pa
(adapted by Eric Whitacr
English translation by Muriel Rukeyse

The poetry of Octavio Paz is a composer's dream. The music seems to set itself (without the usua struggle that invariably accompanies this task) and the process feels more like cleaning the oils from an ancient canvas to reveal the hidden music than composing. *Water Night* was no exceptior and the tight harmonies and patient unfolding seemed to pour from the poetry from the first reading, singing its magic even after the English translation. *Water Night* is simply the natural musical expression of this beautiful poem, and is dedicated with my greatest sincerity to my friend and confidant Dr Bruce Mayhall.

E.V

Commissioned by the 2002 California All-State Choir

A BOY AND A GIRL

for Dr Ron Kean

OCTAVIO PAZ

ERIC WHITACRE

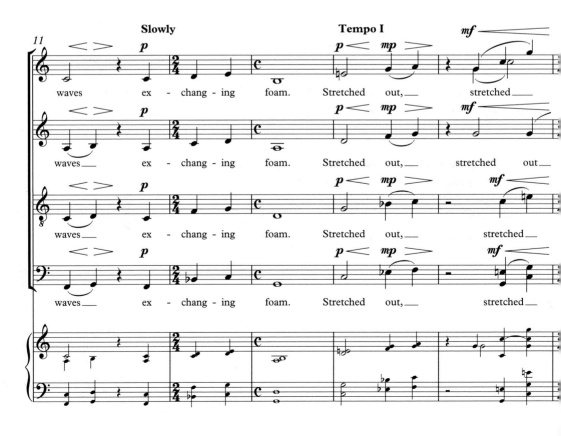

4

noth - ing, nev - er kiss - ing,

noth - ing, nev - er kiss - ing,

noth - ing, nev - er kiss - ing,

noth - ing, nev - er kiss - ing,

giv - ing si - lence for___ si - lence.

giv - ing si - lence for___ si - lence.

giv - ing si - lence si - lence.

giv - ing si - lence si - lence.

6

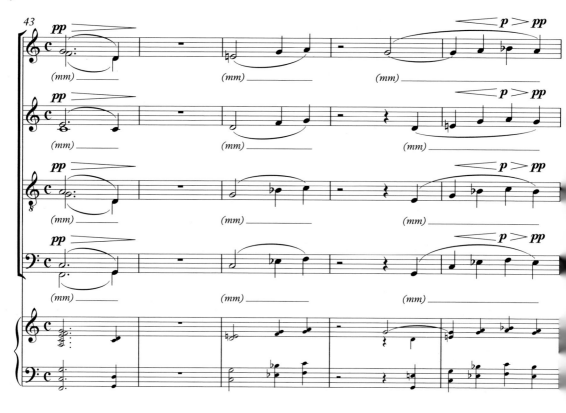

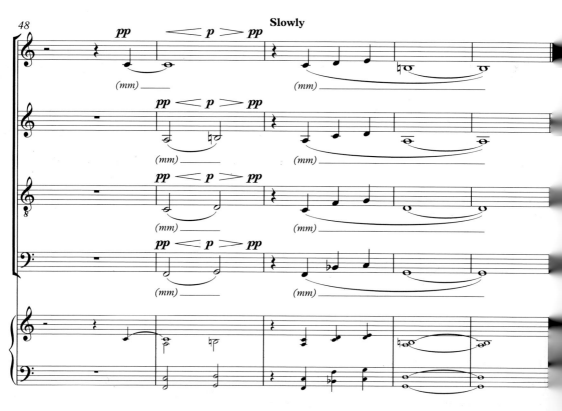

Los Angeles, January 2002

for David B. Weiller and the
University of Nevada, Las Vegas, Chamber Chorale

GO, LOVELY ROSE

EDMUND WALLER

ERIC WHITACRE

* close to *ng*

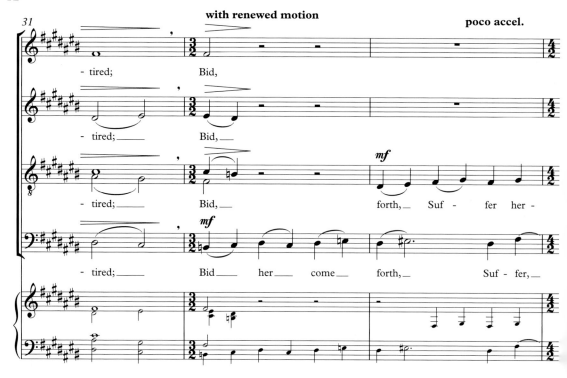

* close to *n* on 2nd beat

14

Las Vegas, August 1991

Commissioned by the Master Chorale of Tampa Bay

15

LUX AURUMQUE
for Dr Jo-Michael Schiebe

EDWARD ESCH
Latin translation by
CHARLES ANTHONY SILVESTRI

ERIC WHITACRE

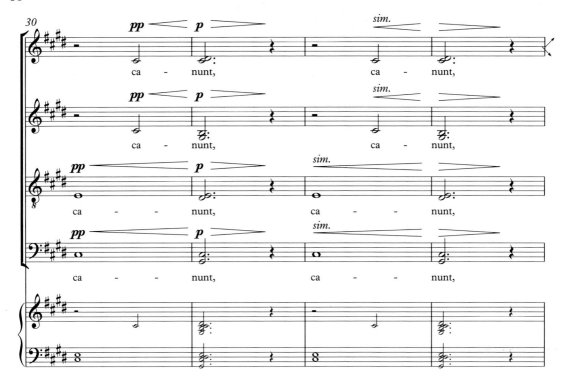

Los Angeles, July 2000

Co-commissioned by VocalEssence, Cora Città di Roma,
Khorikos and Falu Kammarkör

NOX AURUMQUE

dedicated to Philip Brunelle

CHARLES ANTHONY SILVESTRI

ERIC WHITACRE

Ca - nens noc - tis, Ca - nens mor - tis, Ac - qui -

Ca - nens noc - tis, Ca - nens mor - tis

Ca - nens noc - tis, Ca - nens mor - tis Ac -

Ca - nens noc - tis, Ca - nens mor - tis,

-es - cens, ac - qui - es - cens ca - nen - do... Et

Ac - qui - es - cens ca - nen - do... Et

- qui - es - cens ca - nen - do...

Ac - qui - es - cens ca - nen - do...

an - ge - lum___ som - - ni - it au - - ro -
an - ge - lum som - - ni - it au - - ro -
an - ge - lum som - ni - it au - ro -
an - ge - lum som - ni - it au - ro -

Con moto

-ra - rum et bel - lo - rum. Bel - lum!
-ra - rum bel - lo - rum. Bel - lum!
-ra - rum bel - lo - rum. Bel - lum!
-ra - rum bel - lo - rum. Sæ - cu - lo - rum,___ sæ - cu -

24

In - fu - ca - tum tor - pi - dum, au - - rum,
In - fu - ca - tum tor - pi - dum, au - - rum,
In - fu - sca - tum et au - rum,
In - fu - sca - tum et au - rum,

Poco mosso

Su - sci - - ta! Su - sci - -
Su - sci - - ta! Su - sci -
Su - sci - ta! Su - sci -
Su - sci - ta! Su - sci -

* elide to sing as 'brex'

28

rit. poco a poco

Tempo I

-rum, Som - - no - rum. Au - -

-rum, Som - - no - rum. Au - -

-rum, Som - no - rum. Au -

-rum, Som - - no - rum. Au -

-rum, au - - rum, au - -

-rum, au - - rum, au - -

-rum, au - rum, Ca - nens

-rum, au - rum, au -

poco rit.

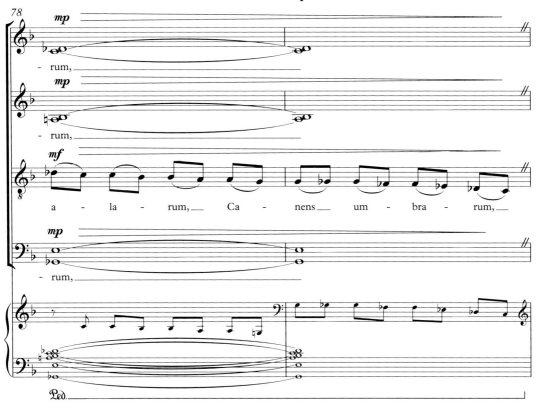

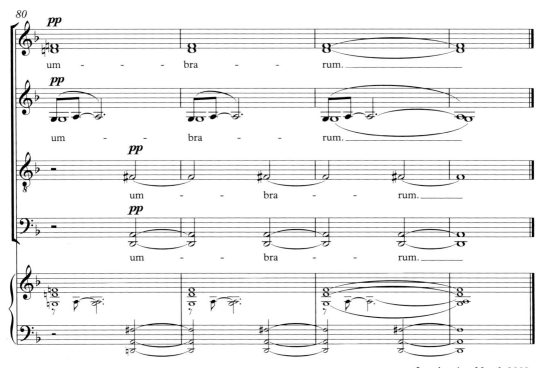

Los Angeles, March 2009

Commissioned in loving memory of Mr M.W. Lacy and Mrs Caroline Morris Lacy
by their daughter Julia Lacy Armstrong

SLEEP

CHARLES ANTONY SILVESTRI

ERIC WHITACRE

Poco più mosso

32

34

Los Angeles, August 2000

Commissioned by *Azusa Pacific University*
for *The APU Chamber Singers, Michelle Jensen, conductor*

THIS MARRIAGE

for Hila on our seventh anniversary

JALAL AD-DIN RUMI

ERIC WHITACRE

May this mar-riage of-fer fruit and shade like the date palm.

May this mar-riage of-fer fruit and shade like the date palm.

May this mar-riage of-fer fruit and shade like the date palm.

May this mar-riage of-fer fruit and shade like the date palm.

May this mar-riage be full of laugh - ter,

May this mar-riage be full of laugh - ter,

May this mar-riage be full of laugh - ter,

May this mar-riage be full of laugh - ter,

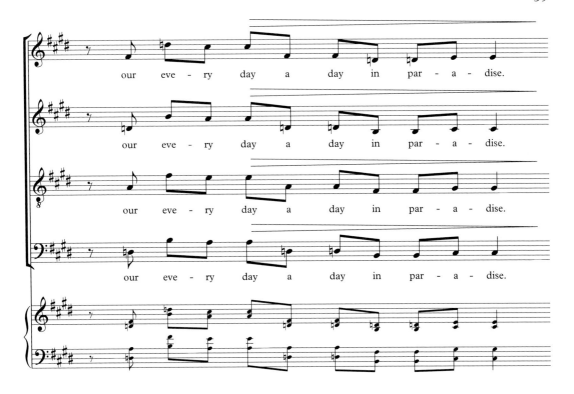

our eve - ry day a day in par - a - dise.

our eve - ry day a day in par - a - dise.

our eve - ry day a day in par - a - dise.

our eve - ry day a day in par - a - dise.

May this mar - riage be a sign of com - pas - sion,

May this mar - riage be a sign of com - pas - sion,

May this mar - riage be a sign of com - pas - sion,

May this mar - riage be a sign of com - pas - sion,

40

an o-men as wel-comes the moon in a clear blue sky.

an o-men as wel-comes the moon in a clear blue sky.

an o-men as wel-comes the moon in a clear blue sky.

an o-men as wel-comes the moon in a clear blue sky.

I am out of words to de-scribe how spi-rit min gles in this

I am out of words to de-scribe how spi-rit min - gles in this

I am out of words to de-scribe how spi-rit min - gles in this

I am out of words to de-scribe how spi-rit min - gles in this

Los Angeles, October 2004

WATER NIGHT

dedicated in deepest friendship to Dr Bruce Mayhall

OCTAVIO PAZ
translated by MURIEL RUKEYSER

ERIC WHITACRE

In all three or four-part women's or men's divisi sections,
there should be a division of voices resulting in a balanced sound.

11

horse that trem - bles, ___ is in your eyes _ of _ se - cret wa - ter.

horse that trem - bles, ___ is in your eyes of se - cret wa - ter.

horse that trem - bles, ___ is in your eyes of se - cret wa - ter.

horse that trem - bles, ___ is in your eyes of se - cret wa - ter.

16 sub. *f* *mp*

Eyes of shad-ow - wa - ter, ___ eyes of well - wa - ter, ___

Eyes of shad-ow - wa - ter, ___ eyes of well - wa - ter, ___

Eyes ___ of shad-ow - wa - ter, eyes of well - wa - ter, ___

Eyes ___ of shad-ow - wa - ter, eyes of well - wa - ter, ___

eyes, night o-pens doors of musk, the se-cret king-dom of the

eyes, night o-pens doors of musk, the se-cret king-dom of the

eyes, night o-pens doors of musk,__ the se - cret

eyes, night o-pens doors__ of musk,__ the se - cret

wa - ter o - pens flow-ing from the cen-tre of the night.

wa - ter o - pens flow-ing from the cen-tre of the night.

king-dom of the wa-ter o-pens flow-ing from the cen-tre of the night.

king-dom of the wa-ter o-pens flow-ing from the cen-tre of the night.

Las Vegas, December 199